This book belongs to

_____

Just Call Me Scholar

Written by Terry Ann Williams-Richard
Illustrated by Lee Johnson

Dedication

This book is dedicated to my daughter Tamara and my grand daughter Peyton Ann. It is also dedicated to my nephew Steven and his daughter, my great niece Amora Rudi. To all my nieces, nephews, great nieces, great nephews, older former students and their children, younger former and current students, and young scholars around the world, this book is also for you.

Just Call Me Scholar

I am articulate, brilliant, courageous, determined, empowered, and free.

People often wonder what they should call me.
Just call me scholar.

I have a unique texture to my hair and a sparkling shine to my skin.

I have royal blood and God's greatness flowing within.

My ancestors and present day elders cloak me with their love it's true.

This casts out the hatred and false information our enemies spew.

"Your future is bright!"
is what my Momma and
Daddy always say.

I am using, building, and sharing my skills, talents, abilities, and gifts every day.

I make a difference in the world, even right now.

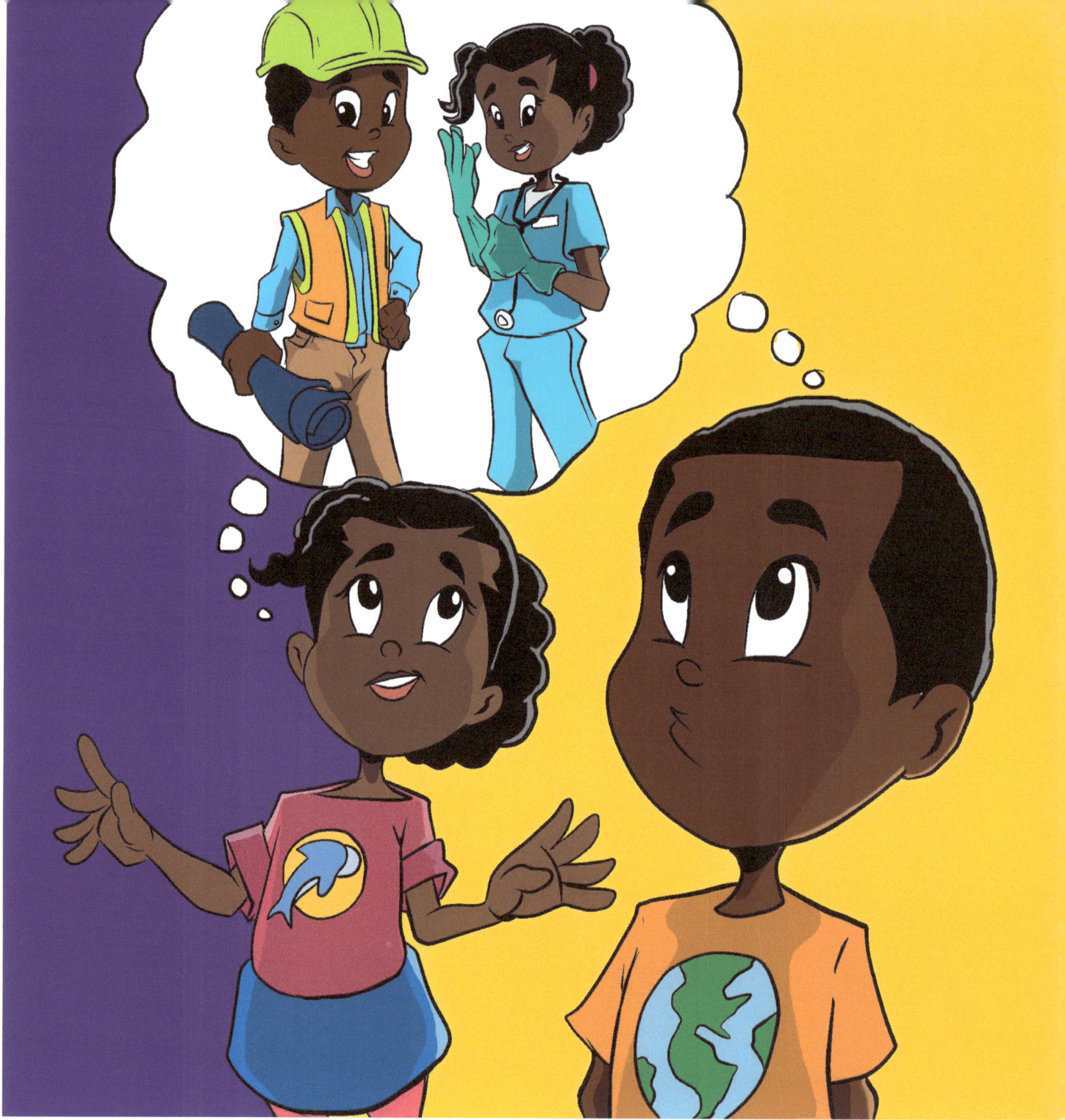

My dreams keep getting bigger. All I can say is, "Wow!"

I am articulate, brilliant, courageous, determined, empowered, and free.

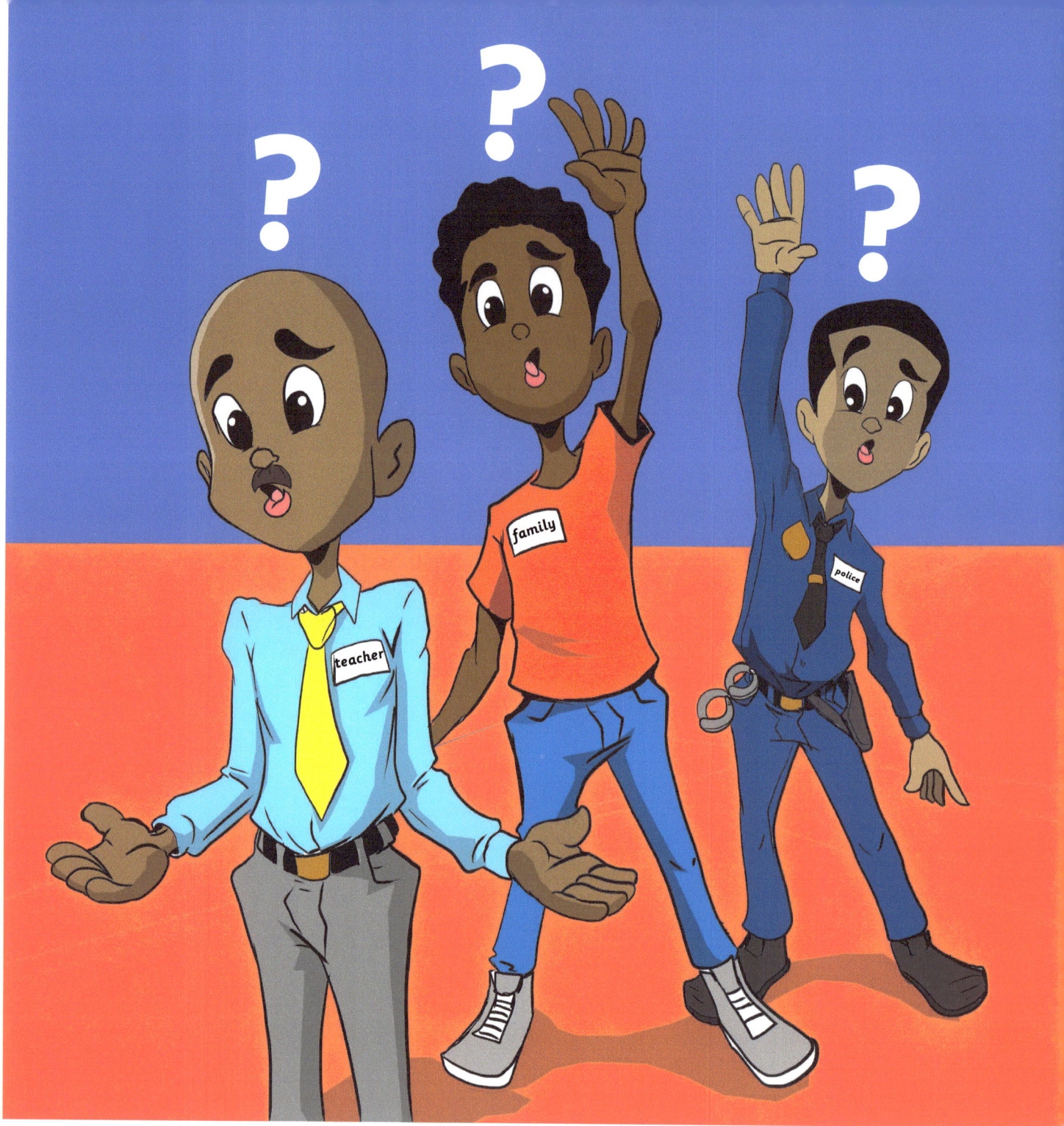

People often wonder what they should call me...

Just call me scholar, that's me!

About the Author

Terry Ann Williams-Richard is committed to encouraging and equipping children to succeed. She is dedicated to empowering young scholars to believe in and walk in their own greatness. Through her programs, instruction, rhymes, talks, and books Ms. Richard inspires students to say "Yes" to success in learning and in life. She is a native of Cincinnati, OH. and enjoys singing karaoke, making up silly songs, writing poetry, attending cultural events, and visiting art museums.

www.ingramcontent.com/pod-product-compliance
Lightning Source LLC
Chambersburg PA
CBHW042009090426
42811CB00015B/1593